Uncommon

Growth

224 Lessons to Help You Live an
Extraordinary Life in a Common World

Stephanie L. Jones
Award-Winning & Best-Selling Author of The Giving Challenge

Uncommon Growth

Copyright © 2023 by Stephanie L. Jones

Scripture quotations are taken from the Holy Bible, New Living Translation, copyright © 1996, 2004, 2015 by Tyndale House Foundation. Used by permission of Tyndale House Publishers, Inc., Carol Stream, Illinois 60188. All rights reserved.

Giving Gal Press books may be ordered by contacting Giving Gal Press, a division of Giving Gal, L.L.C., www.GivingGal.com, 219-707-9545.

Because of the internet's dynamic nature, any web address or links contained in this book may have changed since publication and may no longer be valid.

ISBN: 978-1-948693-12-7

Library of Congress Number: 2023906791

Print information is available on the last page.

Giving Gal Press Date April 2023

Disclaimer and Limit of Liability

To brady, Brionna, Scott, and Tianna,

may you continually work hard, follow your dreams, and remember all the people who love you and support you in Indiana.

Uncommon
Growth

A portion of the proceeds from every copy of *this
book* is donated to
organizations that support education for
underprivileged children.

I appreciate your support!

CONTENTS

INTRODUCTION

Every year around graduation time, I have the idea to write down the lessons I wish I would have learned after graduating high school that led to uncommon growth in my life. The growth led me to adventures, successes, and living a good life, way beyond my wildest dreams.

I knew some of the lessons I mentioned but never grasped their concept or put them into action until later in life.

I love my life and have few regrets, but I could have avoided much hardship if I had implemented these lessons sooner.

Today, May 16, 2021, while reading my Bible, I thought about the upcoming graduation party for my best friend, Amy's, son, Brady.

Amy is my longest friend. We met in kindergarten, and as they say, the rest is history. We have been best friends ever since.

I never had children, so the children of friends and family became part of my life in one way or another. I fill the role of an aunt, often without having the bloodline to prove it.

Brady's graduation party is two weeks away, and I once again am flooded with these lessons I want to pass along to him or anyone needing a little guidance in life.

I grabbed my pen and notebook, and the lessons flowed like water spilling over a waterfall. I could not write fast enough. Within an hour, I'd written this book.

Many of these lessons are not unique. I have just taken the time to jot them down so they can be passed along and given to others.

Many lessons are essential, but I choose to focus on lessons I have a story behind. Like hey, "I lived this, and it works." or, "Learn from my mistake."

Uncommon Growth is written for graduates, but as I read through the list, I realized this book is for anyone who wants to improve their life and live beyond being average, and live the life God created you to live.

Thank you for allowing me to share my insights into what, I believe, leads to *Uncommon Growth*.

LESSONS

LESSON 1

Talk to God every day. Friends will
let you down, but God will not .

LESSON 2

Be grateful. Find five things to be thankful for every day. You will go through tough times, but if you choose to find the good, the weight of your situation will be easier to carry.

LESSON 3

Smile at everyone that crosses your path.

LESSON 4

Don't spend more money than
you make.

LESSON 5

Create a budget and live by it. No matter how little or how much money you have in the bank, your budget should be your guide.

LESSON 6

Call your mom and dad every week. Texting doesn't count.

LESSON 7

Forgive others. Don't worry about their reaction. It's more to lift the weight off of you than them.

LESSON 8

Find one way to make a difference in someone's life daily. Your action doesn't have to be grand. Remember, some of the most impactful gifts you will give will take you little time and cost you no money.

LESSON 9

Give and expect nothing in return,
not even a thank you.

LESSON 10

Don't say I'm sorry if it's not needed.

LESSON 11

Before you judge someone,
remember they may be dealing
with a struggle you know
nothing about.

LESSON 12

Show others grace, including yourself.

LESSON 13

Always give to the homeless, even if it's direct eye contact, a hello, and a smile. They are human, and you are no better than they are.

LESSON 14

Know that money will never make you happy.

LESSON 15

Buy a car that gets you from point A to point B. Invest your money in other areas of your life, such as travel, experiences, others, and your living space.

LESSON 16

While trail running with my dad, I tripped and took a nasty fall. After looking at my scrapes and scratches, I hopped back up and continued running. I complained a bit to my dad, who simply replied, "It doesn't matter that you fell; you got back up." Great advice. Don't focus on the fall, and, if you do fall, get back up!

LESSON 17

Set a goal to read a certain
number of books each year. Books
expand your knowledge, point of
view, and vocabulary and will
improve your writing.

LESSON 18

Give away compliments like candy, even to strangers. Compliments are a simple way to make someone's day and will make your heart smile.

LESSON 19

Don't waste time on social media. If you find yourself scrolling through social media, go back to #17.

LESSON 20

Don't cuss, especially at work and around children.

LESSON 21

Filter the shows and movies you watch and the music you listen to. Ask yourself, is this good for my soul? Is it positive?

LESSON 22

Don't post about politics on social media. It only causes division. Be a uniter. Set a standard of only positing words and comments of encouragement and positivity. You never know who is watching and paying attention to you.

LESSON 23

Always remember what you do and say today may affect a job you want in the future. Therefore, be careful what you or someone else records you doing. Words said in anger or jest will live forever on the internet.

LESSON 24

No job is beneath you. We all have to start somewhere, and the bottom teaches us lessons we will never learn (but will need to know) at the top.

LESSON 25

Always show gratitude to the housekeepers, trash collectors, servers, janitors, and those with often a thankless job. See them and recognize them for their contribution to making our world a better place.

LESSON 26

When you pack up your apartment or home, be ruthless in eliminating what you no longer love or use. Do you want to take the energy to pack, unpack, and find a place for your item?

LESSON 27

When you move into a new apartment or home, unpack immediately and hang pictures on the wall. The longer you draw out the process, the longer you'll have boxes stacked in your house. Which then should remind you of what I recommended in #26. You probably shouldn't have moved the items that are still in boxes months/years later.

LESSON 28

Tip well, even to bad (not rude) servers. You never know what they are dealing with in their lives.

LESSON 29

If you work in customer service,
don't dump your problems on
the customer.

LESSON 30

Respect police officers. If you are pulled over, turn off the vehicle, place your keys on the dash, and put both hands on the steering wheel. Only move your hands when asked to retrieve your driver's license. Before moving your hands, tell the officer the location of where you are reaching. Everyone wants to go home safely. Don't be a jerk.

LESSON 31

Watch sunrises and sunsets any
chance you get.

LESSON 32

Look up, there is often great beauty surrounding us, but we must lift our heads to the sky to see it.

LESSON 33

Change perspective. Don't look at everything from your point of view. For example, if you struggle with a friend, teammate, coworker, or family member, try to see the situation from their perspective.

LESSON 34

God has the perfect person for
you. So don't worry about whom
you are going to marry.

LESSON 35

Don't marry for looks. Make a list of nonnegotiables when it comes to your spouse. Don't lower your standards for good looks or a large bank account.

LESSON 36

Do your best in school but don't stress about grades unless you move on to graduate school or a career that requires good grades. Most likely, your employer won't ask to see your grades.

LESSON 37

Always have a job, even if
you are an athlete or on a
full-ride academic scholarship.
Get in the habit of working,
building your resume, and
earning your own money.

LESSON 38

Listen to a podcast every day.
Always be learning and expanding
your knowledge. Don't know where
to start? Check out my podcast,
Giving Your Best Life!

LESSON 39

Keep a daily journal. No need to write a book; jot down what happened. Events you want to remember. I know you think you'll remember something cool that happened, but trust me, you won't!

LESSON 40

Don't text and drive. No matter how good you think you are at it, you are not. Emily Huntington, a senior in high school, sent one text that cost her her life. It's believed it takes three seconds or less to distract you. No text is worth your life or killing someone else.

LESSON 41

Our actions have consequences.

LESSON 42

Always wear your seatbelt. My dad, a 20-year police officer, told me, "I never pulled a dead body out of a seatbelt."

LESSON 43

Don't drink to fit in. If you want to have a couple of drinks, that's okay, but never drink to the point what you do and say is out of your control. One action that gets recorded can end a future career opportunity.

LESSON 44

Don't try/experiment with drugs. I know this sounds like duh, but I can't tell you how many times I've heard from an addict that it only took them one time doing a drug for them to become addicted.

LESSON 45

Stay hydrated. Continuously sip on water. Water helps you focus and keeps all your organs functioning properly and your skin healthy.

LESSON 46

Don't turn to food for comfort. If you haven't started, don't. You'll fight a lifelong battle if you do.

LESSON 47

When an opportunity to have fun with your friend arises, and you aren't sure you want to participate, ask yourself what my friend Matt, used to ask me, "What are you going to remember in ten years, that you stayed in studying or went out and had fun." And guess what? I chose the fun! My homework/work always got done. This isn't permission to slack off, but you have to have balance in life.

LESSON 48

Friends will come and go. But, those that are important will stay connected to you, and you will be connected to them.

LESSON 49

A conversation is like a ping-pong game. It would be best if you weren't doing all the talking, and neither should the other party.

LESSON 50

Ask questions. Get to know people on a personal, not just surface, level.

LESSON 51

Ask questions of the media and
political figures (on both sides).
Don't take their word for granted.
Be a critical thinker.

LESSON 52

Do your research. Never share content you can't validate through multiple sources.

LESSON 53

When struggling to make a
decision, ask yourself, "What's the
worse thing that can happen?"

LESSON 54

When you have negative thoughts about yourself bouncing around in your head, ask yourself two questions: 1) Is what I'm thinking true?; and 2) Who told me that? These two questions will quickly make you realize the lies you are telling yourself. Unfortunately, most of what we think about ourselves is not valid.

LESSON 55

Don't be afraid of getting the answer of no. People will surprise you. More often than not, they will say yes.

LESSON 56

Pick a weight and size you never want to exceed. I'm 45, and I've been the same size for 20 years. My college weight/size was not reasonable. Some days, my jeans are tighter than others, but it's hard to turn back once you start trending upward on the scale.

LESSON 57

Take baths. They are relaxing, and your problems will float away for a while.

LESSON 58

When you can afford it, get a
massage.

LESSON 59

If a doctor recommends you need
back surgery, find a good
chiropractor, referred by friends,
and get a second opinion.

LESSON 60

Be patient. We live in an instant-results society. Too many people gave up on their dreams, and the calling God laid on their hearts because they were impatient.

LESSON 61

Have a dream list and always add and check items off. The items don't have to be significant. Some call this a bucket list, but I prefer the thought of focusing on living out dreams than kicking the bucket.

LESSON 62

Learn how to flip negative talk to positive talk in your mind and the words you speak. For example, as Coach Mockbee taught me, switch "I can't" to "I can." Small mindset changes can make a powerful shift in your life.

LESSON 63

When traveling, don't eat at chain restaurants. Instead, support the locals and gain new experiences.

LESSON 64

Set priorities. If you have no priorities in life, you'll be pulled in 100 directions. Have three to five priorities and as opportunities, requests, and events come your way, ask yourself, "Does this align with my priorities?" If so, do you have the time or want to make time? If not, what are you willing to sacrifice for something that isn't a priority?

LESSON 65

In December, write down goals for the upcoming year. Make sure they are SMART goals (specific, measurable, attainable, realistic, and timeframe). After you've written your goals, write down the first three actions you need to take to accomplish your goals. Also, write down what obstacles might get in your way. Then, look at your goals every day and take action each week to accomplish them.

LESSON 66

Take off your shoes and socks and stand in the grass. Let your feet soak in the earth. Oh, it feels so good.

LESSON 67

Check your vitamin D levels. Work with your doctor! Get plenty of sunshine or take a supplement if you are low.

LESSON 68

Have a good doctor you trust that focuses on treating the cause of what ails you and not just symptoms.

LESSON 69

Get your teeth cleaned twice a year.

LESSON 70

Floss daily. Better yet, invest in a
Waterpik.

LESSON 71

Don't live with your spouse before
you marry them.

LESSON 72

Tell your friends and family you love them as often as possible.

LESSON 73

Send thank-you notes when you receive a gift or when someone makes a difference in your life.

LESSON 74

When a friend loses a loved one, don't just be there for them in the beginning. Be there for the long haul. Remember important dates. Most people will fade away and return to their lives, but the grief and loss will never go away, for your friend, and neither should you.

LESSON 75

Always have stamps and blank note cards on hand. Never let a moment pass to send a note of encouragement, sympathy, congratulations, or happy birthday to a friend.

LESSON 76

When someone pops into your mind, send them a text saying, "I'm thinking of you. You doing okay?" I can't tell you how many times texts to those I love were sent at the perfect time.

LESSON 77

Have an accountability partner. This person is someone that is invested in you, living out your big dreams. They check in on your goals. They give you tough love. And they are there to make sure you keep moving forward.

LESSON 78

Have a board of directors. When you need to make a big decision in life, seek the counsel of people from various walks of life who have your best interests at heart. You don't have to follow everything they recommend; you need to get input and different views. They will reveal perks, challenges, or issues you may not have considered and give you a different perspective.

LESSON 79

Plan out your week on Sunday nights.

LESSON 80

Have a plan for each day.

LESSON 81

It's okay to let go and distance
yourself from negative people.

LESSON 82

If your significant other ever hits you, seek help immediately. Don't be embarrassed to tell someone. You are stronger than you think you are. Regardless of what your significant other says, after they hit you, it is never your fault. And don't believe them when they say, "It will never happen again." It will. It is easier to leave them now than later. The longer you stay, the harder it is to go. Also, know that leaving is dangerous. Seek support from those you trust; even your local domestic violence shelter can provide guidance.

LESSON 83

Always make your own money.
Know what is going on with your
finances.

LESSON 84

Don't waste money on expensive clothing. Instead, buy what you need and find ways to give clothes to those in need.

LESSON 85

Recycle.

LESSON 86

Don't litter.

LESSON 87

At the store, always return your
cart to the corral.

LESSON 88

Have a morning routine that doesn't involve scrolling through social media or work emails. My prayer and gratitude journal, *Thank-You Notes to God,* may help! Prayer, reading the Bible, writing down five things you are grateful for, stretching, and drinking a glass of water are great ways to start your day.

LESSON 89

Be comfortable going in public
without make-up.

LESSON 90

Less is more.

LESSON 91

Don't shop for therapy or to fill your time. Only go shopping when you have a need and the money to buy what you need.

LESSON 92

Know the difference between a
need and a want.

LESSON 93

Don't use credit cards. If you do,
track your expenditures
meticulously, and pay your bill in full
each month. If you can't pay in full,
don't use them, as the interest they
charge you is exorbitant.

LESSON 94

Eat three veggies and three servings of fruit each day. This may be below the recommended standard, but it's an excellent place to start if you are not used to eating fruits and veggies.

LESSON 95

Get out in nature. Find trails and go for a hike. Turn off the music or noise from your phone and soak in the silence and songs of nature.

LESSON 96

Make a goal and pursue it to travel to all 50 states in the U.S.A. Discover all the wonders this beautiful land has to offer.

LESSON 97

If you travel to a poor, third-world country with sandy beaches and beautiful resorts, make friends with those serving you and tip them well.

LESSON 98

Vote. Men and women died for that right.

LESSON 99

Always stand, place your hand over your heart, and be still for the National Anthem and the Pledge of Allegiance.

LESSON 100

Whenever you see a Veteran, walk up to them, extend your hand, and thank them for their service.

LESSON 101

Pay for someone's food or drink in
the line behind you.

LESSON 102

Enjoy live music.

LESSON 103

Give yourself a day of rest.

LESSON 104

Go on a picnic.

LESSON 105

Participate in events at your local park.

LESSON 106

Support a local fundraiser.

LESSON 107

Have at least one physical goal
each year that will stretch you.

LESSON 108

Shop at farmer's markets and
support local farmers and small
businesses.

LESSON 109

Find a nonprofit and volunteer.

LESSON 110

There is healing power in a comfy
chair, a snuggly blanket, a good
book, and a cup of tea.

LESSON 111

Enjoy and notice the simple things in life.

LESSON 112

Watch squirrels play in the trees. You'll be in awe of what you witness.

LESSON 113

Own a birdhouse and a
hummingbird feeder.

LESSON 114

Always have an extra case, or two, of bottled water.

LESSON 115

When driving, pay attention to your location. Know the crossroads, the direction you are traveling, and the mile marker. You never know when you may need to call for help. Unfortunately, the police can't help if they can't find you.

LESSON 116

If you are traveling in cold temperatures, keep a blanket, warm clothes, food, and water in your vehicle.

LESSON 117

Own a first aid kit.

LESSON 118

Take a C.P.R. course, get
certified, and keep it renewed.
You never know when you might
be at the right place and time to
save a life.

LESSON 119

Every time you gather with friends and family, take pictures.

LESSON 120

Wash and treat a scrape or bug bite immediately.

LESSON 121

Always have a pair of tennis shoes in your car. It will stink if you need to walk to a gas station in heels or flip-flops.

LESSON 122

Trust your gut.

LESSON 123

Don't get in an elevator with a stranger who gives you a bad feeling.

LESSON 124

Celebrate Mondays! Find something from the weekend or upcoming week to celebrate. Celebrating your Mondays will change your mindset and start your week off on the right foot. (Fabulous idea from my bff and Brady's mom, Amy Linkel)

LESSON 125

Wave and smile when someone lets you cut in in heavy traffic. And always allow at least one drive-in in front of you.

LESSON 126

Don't try to fix others' problems.

LESSON 127

If someone opened a door for you in life, find a way to repay them when they least expect it.

LESSON 128

Donate books that are
collecting dust on your shelf to
Little Free Libraries.

LESSON 129

When you have money, children, or possessions of value, get a will. Don't leave your family guessing about your wishes.

LESSON 130

Attend a law enforcement or military funeral. It will be one of the saddest, yet touching, events you will ever witness.

LESSON 131

When you are mad at someone, write them a note expressing all your feelings, and then throw it away. It will make you feel better, yet you won't say something you may regret later.

LESSON 132

No matter how late it is, eat dinner with your spouse/family.

LESSON 133

Fly the American flag at your home.

LESSON 134

If signing a book or movie deal, never give away the rights to your story. Think twice.

LESSON 135

No wimpy, limp-fish, handshakes. You will be amazed at how impressed people will be with a firm handshake.

LESSON 136

Have a journal just for writing down business and product ideas. You never know when you might be in the position to implement one of those ideas.

LESSON 137

Dinner with friends does not have to be extravagant. Be okay with pizza and a cheap glass of wine or a bottle of water.

LESSON 138

Go to your Bible and God for
guidance, not Google.

LESSON 139

Don't listen to the doubters,
naysayers, and haters.

LESSON 140

Be okay with not being perfect.
Jesus was the only perfect person,
and you are not Jesus.

LESSON 141

Forward progress, even a tiny step, is better than no progress. Keep moving forward.

LESSON 142

If you sign up for a race to run it, never walk. Most people quit because they aren't mentally strong. Know the difference between pain from working hard and an injury.

LESSON 143

Always push your chair under the
table when you get up to leave.

LESSON 144

Chew with your mouth closed, and don't talk while eating. It seems simple, but adults do it all the time!

LESSON 145

Don't leave your purse or wallet in the car.

LESSON 146

Grow a garden, at least once in your life, and share the overflow fruits of your labor.

LESSON 147

Learn one new skill a year. (For example, I loved learning to ice skate and to knit.)

LESSON 148

When asked if you want to
round up for a donation to
charity, say yes.

LESSON 149

Always lock your doors and windows.

LESSON 150

Don't hike, run, or walk with earphones on.

LESSON 151

Ask for directions.

LESSON 152

Inquire about how someone is doing and listen to their response. If "fine" doesn't sound "fine," then dig in.

LESSON 153

Pay attention to what a person isn't saying just as much as you do to what they say. If you pay attention, body language will tell you a lot.

LESSON 154

Be okay with saying, "I don't know, but I'll find the answer." No one likes a know it all. People can tell when you don't know what you are talking about. Be honest.

LESSON 155

Be humble.

LESSON 156

Donate blood. If you can't go due
to a health reason or recent travel,
make a monetary donation to the
American Red Cross.

LESSON 157

It's okay to go to counseling.

LESSON 158

It's okay not to be okay.

LESSON 159

Crying is good for the soul. So never apologize for crying when the moment moves you.

LESSON 160

Wash your sheets.

LESSON 161

If you feel stressed, need to process your thoughts, or just a change of scenery, go on a prayer walk. I love to walk outside, no phone, and chat with God. He's a good listener, and I always feel better after our talks.

LESSON 162

Own a comfy robe and pair
of slippers.

LESSON 163

For any money you receive, give at least 10% away.

LESSON 164

Surprise people with "just because" gifts.

LESSON 165

Remember that Christmas isn't about gifts, decorations, and lights.

LESSON 166

Be okay with not being busy. Being busy is overrated and will wipe you out.

LESSON 167

Take your birthday off work.

LESSON 168

Learn to be comfortable with being alone.

LESSON 169

Take a solo trip each year.

LESSON 170

Never worry about likes and followers. Instead, focus on making a positive difference to one person through what you post.

LESSON 171

Don't compare yourself to others.
God has a plan designed
specifically for you and only you!

LESSON 172

You are always loved.

LESSON 173

Stay in your lane. (That's from my friend Paul Hora. He's right!)

LESSON 174

Never underestimate a good movie
and a bowl of popcorn.

LESSON 175

Learn to boil water and cook
noodles to perfection.

LESSON 176

Pay attention to the ingredients in the products you buy and the food you eat. The fewer the ingredients, the better.

LESSON 177

Know the difference between confidence and arrogance and act accordingly.

LESSON 178

Take risks. Don't be scared of rejection. The more you put yourself out there, the more opportunities there are for success.

LESSON 179

Stand up for yourself.

LESSON 180

Stand up for people who are
bullied.

LESSON 181

Be okay with not going with
the flow.

LESSON 182

Don't talk to hear yourself talk. Do that long enough, and people will tune you out.

LESSON 183

Don't expect a handout. Earn every dime you have, respect that is given, and your education/career.

LESSON 184

Mentor a student who is behind
you in class/grade/career but
wants to do what you are doing.

LESSON 185

Over-prepare for an interview
and ask questions of the
interviewer.

LESSON 186

Don't be late—respect
others' time.

LESSON 187

Let others speak. Don't interrupt.

LESSON 188

Check the inside of your shoes for bees, spiders, and bugs before you put them on.

LESSON 189

Chat with people in elevators. And when you exit, tell them to have a fabulous day! It will make them smile.

LESSON 190

Always have a half tank of gas. If you are traveling a long distance, take the time to fill up your tank.

LESSON 191

In your dorm room, apartment, or home, surround yourself with pictures of friends and family, your favorite quotes, and Bible verses. Always be able to look and fill your mind with positive thoughts.

LESSON 192

Don't order online out of impulse. Instead, put an item in your cart and return several days later. Ask yourself, "Do I need this item?"

LESSON 193

Don't gamble your hard-earned
money. The house always wins.

LESSON 194

Save for big purchases and
vacations. If you can't afford it,
don't buy it.

LESSON 195

Visit family and friends when you can, not when it is convenient. It will never be convenient.

LESSON 196

Keep up family traditions.

LESSON 197

Create traditions.

LESSON 198

When you leave home, always give hugs, kisses, and say, "I love you."

LESSON 199

If you go through a difficult
time, ask God, "What lessons
do you want me to learn?" And
then pay attention.

LESSON 200

If you want an excuse, you will find one.

LESSON 201

Give love and money freely to those that need it. Don't be greedy or stingy.

LESSON 202

Remember, if you work hard, you'll always make more money.

LESSON 203

Lead with a compassionate heart.

LESSON 204

Are you going through a hard time? Remember, there is someone that always has it worse than you do.

LESSON 205

"Jump in puddles and get your shoes dirty." Coach Bullock

LESSON 206

Run in the rain.

LESSON 207

Watch the sky for severe weather.

LESSON 208

Sometimes when you hear no, it's God's way of protecting you.

LESSON 209

There is a difference between no and not now. Be patient.

LESSON 210

Walk through open doors.

LESSON 211

Change is good. If we avoid
change, we miss the opportunities
to grow.

LESSON 212

Usually, when people hate on you, it has more to do with their issues than you. Love those people, even when it is hard.

LESSON 213

If you have a disability, don't use it to limit yourself or as an excuse. A blind man has climbed Mount Everest. You can do more than you believe.

LESSON 214

Listen when people speak, but only take advice from people who have been there and done that.

LESSON 215

Sometimes the "experts" are wrong.

LESSON 216

Don't drag out a relationship because you are scared of hurting the other person. The longer you linger, the harder it will be to leave.

LESSON 217

If you tell people you will pray for them, actually pray for them. Write it down, snap a picture, and text it to them. Or, if you are with them, grab their hand, and pray with them at the moment. All three are powerful and impactful.

LESSON 218

Don't just go to God in prayer when you are in trouble. Instead, get in the habit of thanking Him for the big and small things in your life. Seek forgiveness as often as you need it.

LESSON 219

Don't poo-poo other's dreams. (I can remember telling my dad, "One day, I'll be a millionaire." Without hesitation, he replied, "I have no doubt you will.")

LESSON 220

In a business deal, no matter how much you trust the person, always get a signed contract.

LESSON 221

Be careful with whom you share your crazy big dreams/goals. (I can't tell you how many times I got excited about a project or idea, and shared it with someone, and they deflated my enthusiasm, made me doubt myself, and sometimes killed a project. I'm now very cautious about whom I share my idea with, and often I don't share a project with anyone until I'm far enough along that I know I won't let them derail me.)

LESSON 222

Be bold in your actions. Pursue and
live out your big dreams. Bless
others in everything you do.

LESSON 223

Most of what you fear will never
come true. Be courageous!

LESSON 224

Remember...Jesus loves you (and so do I)!

I hope you enjoyed reading the list of lessons as much I have loved walking down memory lane and compiling them for this book. I will warn you, these lessons do you no good if you don't go out and put them in practice. Refer back to this book often. Where it fits in your life, make it a goal to tackle, one lesson a week. Maybe it's giving a gift every day or writing out what you are grateful for. Maybe you are scared to take a step of faith, well my friend, be courageous! No matter where you go from here, remember you can go out and live an extraordinary life!

I would love to hear from you. What lesson are you tackling? What lesson would you add? Maybe I'll write Uncommon Growth Part II and include your advice. If you are on social media, share what lesson you are tackling and advice using #UncommonGrowth. Let us all grow together!

LET'S CONNECT!

Website and blog: www.GivingGal.com and www.GivingYourBestLife.com

Facebook: www.facebook.com/GivingGal

Join our Facebook Group: www.facebook.com/groups/givingyourbestlife

Instagram: @Giving_Gal

LinkedIn: www.linkedin.com/in/StephanieLeeJones

Podcast: Giving Your Best Life (wherever you listen to podcasts)

Children's books: www.givinggalbooks.com

Need a speaker for your next event?

I love speaking on giving, gratitude, goals, my experiences as a police wife, and leadership. If you need a speaker for your next conference, fundraiser, church service, retreat, school, workshop, or business meeting, I am your gal!

If you have questions, want to share a story, or need giving ideas, drop me an email at Stephanie@GivingGal.com.

I would love to hear from you!

With gratitude,

Stephanie

THE PERFECT GIFT

Grab a piece of paper and make a list of people in your life who could benefit from *Uncommon Growth*, or my other books, such as a friend, coworker, family member, graduate, Sunday school class, or your small group. My books make a perfect gift for all occasions and all ages. You can purchase copies at www.GivingGal.com/Shop. Email Stephanie@GivingGal.com for bulk purchases.

DYSLEXIA RESOURCE

My first book, *The Giving Challenge*, was a labor of love. I never set out to write a book or share my journey. I wanted to make a difference, me as one person to one person each day. What I found was that choosing to give daily made a difference to thousands of people. I realized that we could change the world and share positive stories that inspire others to go out and do good.

When I started writing *The Giving Challenge*, I was not a writer. I hated writing. I battled God every day, crying a river of tears. I quit numerous times, which took four to five years to publish the first edition. I did not want to write that book. Not only did I hate writing, but when I did write, it was terrible. I had poor grammar. And I can't spell worth a darn. But with all those excuses, I learned to be obedient and not rely on my strengths but trust in God and have faith.

But something happened after I sent my first book out into the world. Right before I released The Giving Challenge, I received a dyslexia diagnosis. A weight I carried for years lifted off my shoulders in an instant. As I shared in this book, I struggled most of my life in silence. I fell in love with writing.

A firehose of stories and book ideas have flooded my mind ever since. I sincerely hope that if you've read both of my books, you'll see improvement in my writing.

Because like anything, if we work at the craft, we can improve. I now attend writer's conferences and work with great editors to learn and grow. I even dream of speaking at writer's conferences, sharing my journey with other writers to encourage them to take a step of faith and share their stories with the world.

If you have a book in you but don't know where to start, I'm here to help. Reach out to me at Stephanie@GivingGal.com, and let's chat about the next step you need to take to see your book on a bookshelf.

P.S. I shared my dyslexia story with you as you may have dyslexia and do not know it. Or maybe you do know and need a little encouragement. Perhaps there is a child in your life who finds reading and writing challenges. Please do not ignore them. They are smart. They only need to learn differently. Get the help. If you don't know where to start, connect with my dear friend Joellyn Hartley at www.JoellynHartley.com. She changed my life, and I know she can do the same for you or a child in your life.

ACKNOWLEDGMENTS

To the graduates of 2021, you've had a rough go over the past couple of years, but our difficulties only make us stronger. I'm so proud of you, Blake, Brady, and Zoe.

Special thanks to:

Mike, my husband—thanks for always supporting my crazy ideas. I love you!

The Giving Your Best Life Facebook group for cheering me on and supporting my book writing endeavors.

My friends, Bethany, and Michelle, at Platinum Literary Service. I am grateful God connected us first on social media and then in person. You help me put out better books.

My editor Boyd Lanier, Ph. D. *Uncommon Growth* is reader-worthy because of you.

My readers, faithful followers, family, and friends— thank you from the bottom of my heart for all your love, support, and big cheers from the sidelines. There is never a minute I forget it is because of you I can live out my dream and consider myself a successful author. I love you all!

To anyone that has taught me one of these life lessons, thank you!

If you want to continue your growth journey, check out my other books:

The Giving Challenge

The Gratitude Challenge

Thank-You Notes to God

Giving Gal

Giving Gal & The Christmas

Cookie Extravagana

Uncommon Christmas